Pro-poets-gress

Albanian Finnatics

Dedicated to: Julie Alba, Dr. Jerry Arganbright, Mr. Finn, and
Iowa City West High School

ICCSD

To Love a Stranger
By: Suha

She nursed her first true love
A new life she created
Pride.
Wailing,
blurred vision, laugh slurred.
Beating heart increased
unleashed warmth inside.
She held it tight, not believing the sight.
Stranger so light, and small.
A new type of happiness.

Held in the warm embrace.
in grace it lays.
curled hands, rest.
Face nest on warm chest
Rosy pink lips.
Shut are oversized eyes,
lashes spread upon flushed cheeks.
Mother leaks with warm love.
Stranger she truly loves.
the length of her forearm, it gloves.
She lays there calm,
dwelling on the day it calls her "mom"

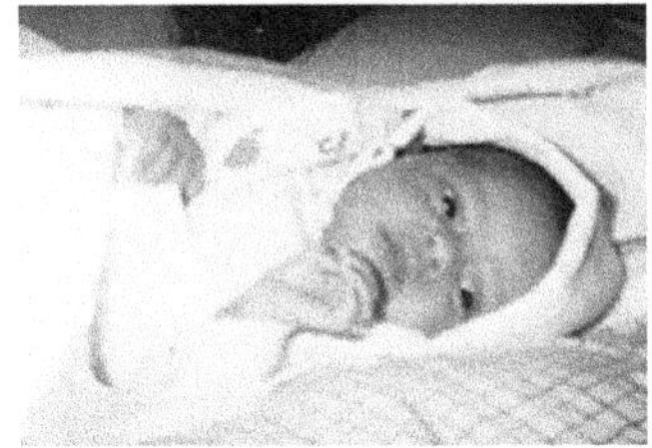

Mine

By: Suha

I need you,
like fish needs water
like a sunny day needs the sun
and like the sun needs the sky
I will cry for you, like a baby cries for his mom
like a mom cries for her son
like a son cries for love
I need you like Ben needs Jerry, and just like Jerry needs Tom
Yet I don't understand why I need you
Just like I don't understand why Tom needs Jerry, when there are other mice to catch
Or why Ben needs Jerry, when it could just be Ben
Since Jerry already has Tom
Why do I need you when I could need somebody else
Yet I will cry for you, like a body cries for a soul
like a soul cries for a body
Because everyone needs a soul, and a body,
just like everyone needs somebody
And you are my somebody
I need you because everyone has you
like everyone has a heart.
like everyone has a mind
But I really don't mind,
because you will eventually be mine.
But...
How do I need you?
If... I don't even know you

The Storm

Corrinne Warnke

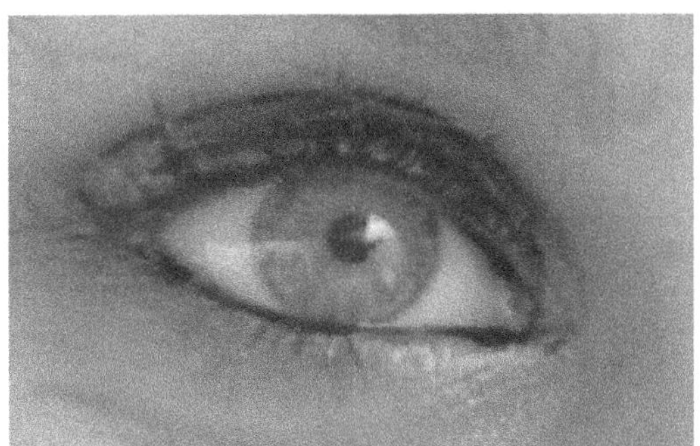

My eyes cannot withhold
the storm that engulfs my heart
clouds fallings over my mind
and slowly fill up my heart
drop by drop I slowly fall
splashing onto the flood
the thunder, the lightning, the waves
slowly drowning my world
as I try to keep my mind afloat
but my heart is an anchor
as it drags me down
into the cold dark depths
of the storm that has engulfed me

Yellowstone Night

By Lydia Rhomberg

Dandelions swim thru delicate wind,

Spreading bliss all around,

Needles flow in the breeze,

Brewing gossip in the air,

Coyotes dance in the moonlight,

Howling in pure darkness,

Calling out to the endless abyss,

Stars flutter in the starry galaxy,

As the pumpkin faces to the pond,

Foot hair

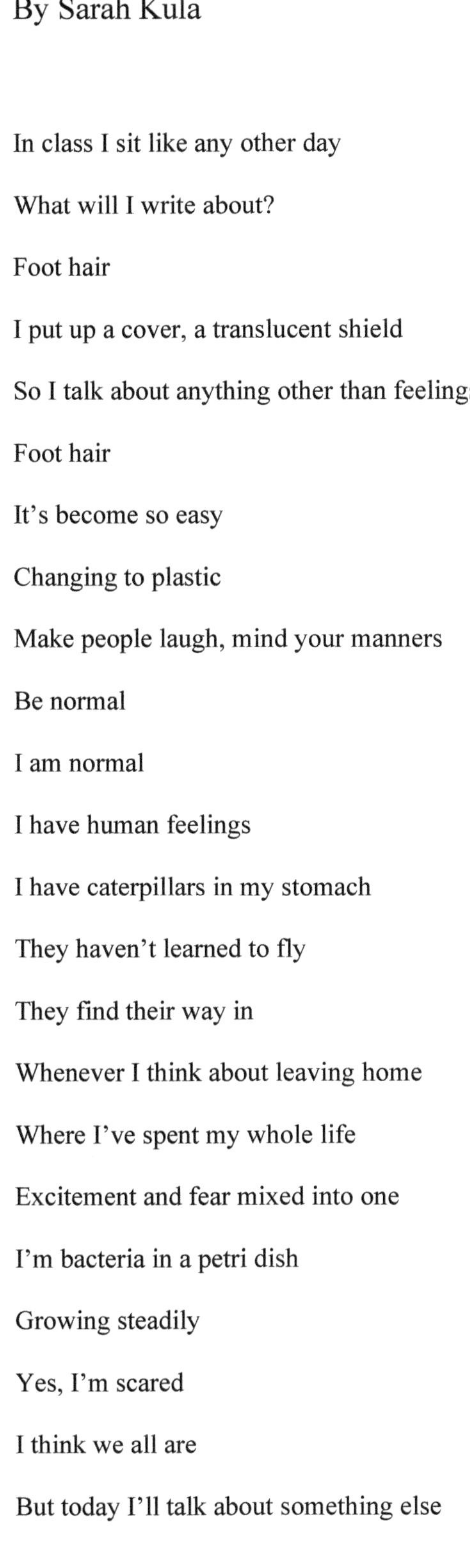

By Sarah Kula

In class I sit like any other day

What will I write about?

Foot hair

I put up a cover, a translucent shield

So I talk about anything other than feelings

Foot hair

It's become so easy

Changing to plastic

Make people laugh, mind your manners

Be normal

I am normal

I have human feelings

I have caterpillars in my stomach

They haven't learned to fly

They find their way in

Whenever I think about leaving home

Where I've spent my whole life

Excitement and fear mixed into one

I'm bacteria in a petri dish

Growing steadily

Yes, I'm scared

I think we all are

But today I'll talk about something else

Like foot hair

Does my reflection show who I really am?

By Kristian McCullough

I'm not sure
If I'm the girl you want
I'm not sure
If what you see in me,
Is the same as what I see in you

I'm no princess bride in pink
Or a golden treasure to find

Don't get me wrong
I'm still a girl
But I'm not sure if I'm the girl you want

I take pride in my sports
Like a man does to his beer
Or to his trophy of a deer hanging high on his wall

I attract dirt so badly
You'd think I'm a vacuum
Every time I'm seen by my mother it's
"Honey, why don't you go find the bathroom?"

My mother tried to change me
But that was a mistake
It was a mistake
Based on a risk, she really couldn't take.

All the sap and love
It's like acid to my skin and face
I like action
The rapid pulse of my heart

CHICAGO
BEARS

My Significant Perpetual High

By Kristian McCullough

Please let me be.
All I want is to be free.

Fine. Don't let me be.
But I'll find a way.

Now before you go thinking negatively
I don't need alcohol or that 'Magical Cannabis'

You see, my perpetual high and escape is different.
I like to read.
And I love to write.

Give me a pen and a piece of paper
I'll write my way to heaven and beyond.

All this wishing and imagining
Is driving me crazy!

How come you won't let me be?
I told you all I want is to be free
To be the person I am
To. Be. Me.

How does it feel to escape?
Writing for minutes, hours even days at a time.
It's a feeling of being in a haze.

A haze that I can control
To fill the void and empty hole.

Kitty Cat

By Karl Ratner

It comes

On little feet

It's far to gaze

Over the horizon of the city

On silent moves

It stalks

My cat on the window

Las Vegas Boulevard

By Lydia Rhomberg

wind scrunches thru Mandalay Bay,

tonight is a new moon,

festival flappers waltz the street in Vegas,

parading the fluorescent boulevard as the moon ascends,

hours glide by, boozed mortals stride the rocky pavement,

sunshine looms above the architecture,

becoming aggravating to the drunks,

as the day goes on, folk make their way towards casinos,

ordering fresh roasted coffee and a hash brown,

retreating back to their hotel rooms,

getting ready for the big day ahead,

the day goes on, and the routine stays constant,

for the next three-hundred-sixty-five- days

On the Spot
Haley Schneider

On the spot
Time ticking by
While the...

Mind is poisoning self when,
Self should be helping mind

Second guessing yourself
You should be assuring

Panicked, weighed in the spot,
Where you should be floating

The air is filled with moisture
It's hard to breathe water

Wading through a swamp
Yeah, that would be easier

Easier than encountering,
Looking in the eye

Staring down a monster,
Yeah, that would be easier

Easier than being criticized
A thousand judging beams on one face

Yeah, that would burn a hole
Right on the Spot

Green Guts of Glory

By Evan Cameron

The blood

It floods

From I80 of Iowa

To the streets of California

The green guts of glory

They rot in the moldy old rock quarry

The fallen brains

And as it rains

Thy heart beats slowly

Yet so unholy

And at 6 feet under

I can still hear the thunder

As it strikes

The shit-smell-stench
like burnt out motor-bikes

The green guts of glory

They smell poorly

Like the one who lies

You watch as it dies

That's what makes you lovely

Like the green guts of glory!!!!

First day

Jordin Robles

We meet that sunny day; everything in my mind went quiet

I just wanted to hug you

I just wanted to see you

I just wanted be with you

Suddenly you surprised me from behind hugging me so hard!

That amazing feeling, I felt butterflies in my stomach everything was different when I was by your side.

That amazing day we spent together.

The time had gone like a thunderbolt,

That tornado comes to me when we said goodbye!

Blind

Sidney Petitgout

roses are a deep bloody flesh red

violets are a deep under sea blue

the sky is a road that doesn't end

while you lay in the grass

the sisters of knifes

rubbing on your skin, making it tickle

as though you're seeing your grandpa for the first time in a while

and he attacks you

giving you something to laugh about again

the trees blow in the wind

like god is taking a deep breath out

even though you can't see

imagine

DARKNESS By: Evan Cameron

The darkness swirls strong like a whirlpool
Evil pressures in my heart
My veins expand like branches
I'm on the edge of detonating
It's as if the weight of the world was upon my shoulders
So powerful like an avalanche
Boulders will make you into road kill
Like rolling thunder we will clash as if we were fighting rams head bashing
And in the end blood will fall like red velvet rose petals
Earth will endure a new darkness
A pitch black fog will engulf the universe
It might be too late to save the world
But in the distance a light glimmers
It's the last sign of hope for this wasteland
One willing heart bright enough to see this through
A new start has Arrived!

Passion

By Jordin Robles

I'm normal person
When it comes to soccer
I'm a different person
I'm in the defense position when I stand in the grass and yelling cheering crow
My heart start beating fast
There is only one person I really notice in the field
It's the yelling of my coach
When I go for the ball
I think of making my coach proud of me
When I stop the ball from getting a goal I feel proud in my self
When it's all over I walk to the car with my ball covered in mud
In my hand I receive compliments saying good game
I feel proud of me

Grandpa

By Marisah Richards

I miss you; I love you; I wail for you; I mourn for you; I cherish the little that I still have from you. I dream of a field with luscious vibrant grass swaying as the wind gently kisses each blade. The field is full of daffodils; vibrant yellows, oranges, whites and pinks cloak each delicate petal. The daffodils have long elegant green legs that extend into delicate fingers of green. The sky is a deep shade of blue that only can be your eye color. I wake up face moist with warm and salty tears. I wail for you like an ambulance that is carrying a women in labor. I reach out for you in the darkness, the only thought I have is to be held by you. I reach, scream, and cry but you don't arrive to save me. It is hard to accept that you are gone, never again to open those beautiful blue eyes, smile with those glistening white teeth, to grace those with your rumbling laughter, never again to embrace me with your strong arms, and to never say "Marisah I love you." I miss you like a hungry child misses the comfort of being full. My stomach turns, my palms get sweaty, and eyes water, mouth quivers, body shivers but most of all my heart shrivels up from missing you. I love you more than a fat man loves food. When I think of you, I can't help but smile so big that it hurts, my heart swells with your love, I'm in a state of pure bliss, my body tingles with joy, and I swell with the feeling of love; love for you, love for me, love from me to you, and love from you to me. I tenderly say goodbye to you. I reflect on all of the memories we made, I memorized the last word's you said, I remember you being sick and frail. I remember how you went downhill fast, like a snowball with every little inch you gradually got sicker and sicker, until your last labored breath escaped from your thin, dark pink, chapped lips. I brush the coffin with the tips of my fingers like a man who is brushing a women's hair from her face. I sit like a British Palace Guard as the funeral service is occurring. I mourn for you, like a country mourning for their king who just passed away. I love you grandpa, to the moon and back with all of my heart.

Freedom

By Kaz Kishiue-Koval

A teenager just turning 16.

Going to the DOT and getting their license.

That feeling they get when

They can drive alone for the first time.

It's like a bird jumping from the nest

And flying for the first time.

Or like dropping a 50 pound bag

After carrying it around for months.

It can bring joy like getting something

That you've wanted for a long time.

This is what getting you driver's license feels like.

Suffer in Silence
By Corrinne Warnke

We suffer in silence
as the seasons change
as the days go by
as the clock ticks
a minutes at a time
and we continue to
hold the pain inside

a girl suffering
mouth sewn shut
drops of pain flooding out
and flowing down
as she rips her mind apart
searching for a light of hope
only finding the darkness of despair

Mental toughness
By Aaron Stumpf

The last sprint, sweat dropping,
face burning, legs hurting.
It feels like 100 degrees
And all I hear is stop and go.
And all I am thinking is one more.

Past but not Past

By Aaron Clinkenbeard

Looking back, I hate it

Forward thinking player

Way to fucking lazy

Drive myself crazy

Considering mistakes

Held down by my own chain

I made it from my own pains

Silt scraping rock down to silt

Etching present back to past

Never letting you move fast

Break chains, wash ashore

Such struggle too hard,

Rinsing and repeating,

Scraping off the future.

Raw Swag Ratchet
By Aaron Clinkenbeard

Why walk away while witnessing horrors?
Six year olds rummaging through toxic waste.
American company labels, wearing away too slow for innocence.
Ignoring the millions whose lives are crushed
Who get up everyday for 16 hours of weaving through blades
threatening limbs and life.
Society agrees, quelling the rational guilt.
Murder, and child abuse known as not okay,
when you don't see anything happen, you won't take the blame
But if you are the cause of a 8 year old Thai
girl's arm being ripped off, a 19 year old Chinese factory worker leaping to her death unable to deal with her life anymore hoping to find something better.
You feel no guilt for their circumstances.

If it cannot be pinned on you, nothing is your fault, but you cannot
pledge innocence by staying neutral, Switzerland.
You cannot say the phone you just threw away did not
come at the price of blood.
You cannot defend your actions, so instead..
You feign ignorance of how fortunate you truly are.
Foreign policy seems so vague.
rights are so easily violated without apparent consequences..
We all stand on a pedestal carried by distant atlas'.
No one cared about atlas, until he shrugged.

Mom's Garden

By Karl Ratner

I have upturned the soil
By sweat and blood I work
Oxygen pumping through my sun-burnt body

The soil bears life
A smell, a feel a sight
Bursts through doe's life
To see the sun

Are You Ok?
By Hannah Birt

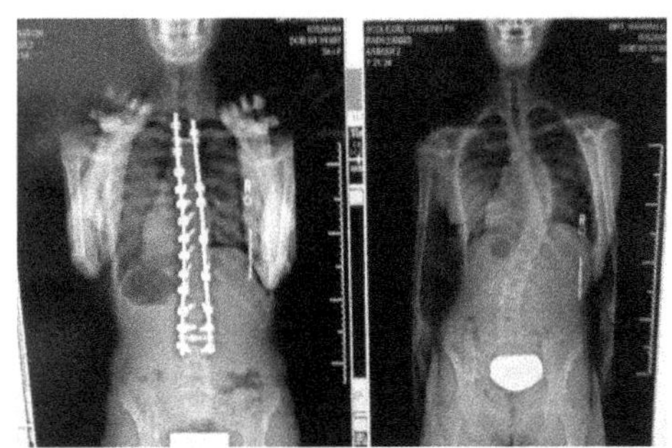

"Is your back okay?"
Slowly, I pivot around to face the offender.
Plastered smile, vacant eyes.
Kind words spoken by a black heart.
Typical.
Answers flip through my head like pictures on a slot machine.
Never settling on quite the right reply.
It's not OKAY that people treat me like I am damaged goods.
It's not OKAY that I can't do a sit-up.
It's not OKAY that I will forever sit up straight.
It's not OKAY that I struggle to open a bottle of water because I never fully got my strength back.
It's not OKAY that everything is twice as hard for me.
It's not OKAY that I spent sometimes four hours a day relearning just how to pass a volleyball, something I had spent five years perfecting.
It's not OKAY that seven years of work in the gym was gone with a few quick slices to my back.
It's not OKAY that I have a seventeen-inch scar on my back that makes moms gawk at the pool.
It's not OKAY that in got so small that my mother can wrap her fingers around my shoulder because I dropped ten pounds when I had nothing to lose.
It's not OKAY that I spent my summer sitting in a hospital bed instead of lounging poolside.
It's not OKAY that my mother has to tie my laces each morning.
It's not OKAY that I have back pain like an old man when I am not even a woman.
It's not OKAY that I had to retake my first steps again at fourteen, re-learning to walk with foreign metal rods inside of me.
And it's definitely not OKAY that I spent 180 days being cared for like a person in hospice instead of a freshman in high school.
But the asker doesn't want to hear any of that.
It takes every ounce of strength in my rod-ridden body for me to push out,
"I am O.K."

Jack

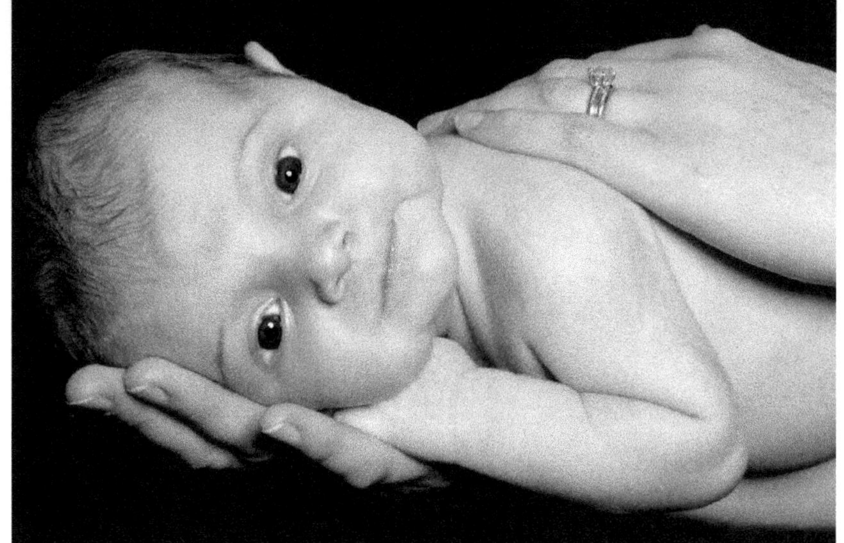

By: Hannah Birt

I used to think that love at first sight was a myth.

Somewhere up with dragons, mermaids and wizards.

I now know that it's real.

The way his brilliant baby blues shone.

His milky completion, flawless.

The crinkles in his dark hair, like a calm tide.

How his tiny hands grasped my fingers, so tightly,

as if he was promising to never let go.

The smirk plastered on his face as if I just whispered him a secret.

But, as I peered down at him in my arms.

I knew I could never love him more than I did right then.

baby brother.

Will I go to Heaven

By Kendra Law

Will I go somewhere?
Will the blue in my veins red
Will the blood at rest knock my chest
Will the buds if pink bloom my cheeks
Will I climb and will I fall
Will the heavens hum
Will there be the sound of drums
Will the gates be shut
Will I be left to the mutts
Swirling flames
Screaming names
Stuck, stuck, stuck.
Forever it seems
Forever it will be
Will I fall to my knees
Will I scream to be free
Will I jump high
From the one i despise
But remember, we're stuck
Will I raise my hands
Will I praise the heavenly bands
Will I be showered in blood
Will his blood rub
I will now say, not ask
I'm going somewhere
I won't go with the rest

The pain of losing
By Aaron Stumpf

Losing is like the pain you fell after being punched
Losing is like stubbing your toe and wanting to scream and swear.
Losing is the difference from first and second
Losing can cause mental breakdown and can cause more losses
But in reality losing is a part of life.
Only a few people can say they are undefeated or unbeaten.

MY CAT
By Lane Dubrock

I feel the warmth of his fur and the quick heartbeats resonating from his chest.
He buries his face into his food bowl while I fill it up.
He walks so close to my legs I almost step on him in the morning waiting for his breakfast.
Sometimes I wonder why he stays with us.
Is it because we feed him or does he realize that he's a part of the family?
He could easily just leave and never come back, so why doesn't he?

FRUSTRATION
By Lane Dubrock

Frustration is a very annoying emotion.
I feel like punching a wall.
It eats away at you until you want to scream.
If anyone is nearby, I will unconsciously let my anger out on them.
It fills up your chest and squeezes it together.
It is very difficult to calm down after being frustrated.

Start from Scratch

By David Jenkins

I wish I could start from scratch like a new born baby

Looking in the mirror like self looking at me like self looking at me like mirror's reflection.

If I could rewind the hands of time I'll go back to when I was 9

Experiencing life like a trailer wondering when to come out

I'll give my own life like I changed God's mind

They say I was a cool cat like I had 9 lives

I have a confession like breaking news

Confession coming soon.

“Lucky”
By Shea Yamashita

Oh Baby. Damn.
I am so lucky to have a girl like you.
I just wish we could see each other more often, you know?
I miss you. A lot. I miss you to the moon and back.
I miss you like an owner misses his dog,
like the dog misses the cat,
like the cat misses the mouse
and the mouse misses the cheese!
… unless he’s lactose intolerant …
Then i guess the mouse doesn’t miss cheese…
I miss you like a mouse doesn’t miss a mouse trap.
Like Tom misses Jerry, like Bob misses Larry, like Sally misses Harry,
there’s something about you like there’s something about Mary,
and i would marry you.
But i can’t…
Which makes me sad.
I know that you’re busy, you’ve got things to do.
You’ve got a life and i’ve got one too.
I just want you in my life more.
I was told we go together perfectly.
Like a cookie and milk,
like a road and silk,
like a shovel and dirt,
like a locker and hurt,
like ernie and bert,
but not like ice cream and sherbert, because sherbert is awful, honestly who would mix fruit and milk,
that’s kind of gross, especially rainbow sherbert.
We go together like cats and dogs,
like bulls and frogs,
like old men trying to get in shape and jogs,
like car accidents and fog,
like cabins and logs,
like egg and nog.
I think you might be the best thing that’s ever happened to me.
Oh baby. Damn.
I’m so lucky to have a girl like you.

Untitled
By Sarah Kula

Crisp crunch of leaves
Heat bouncing off the pavement like a trampoline
Leash stretch out like an old worn toy
greedily begging for more
A sudden jerk
Ears reaching to touch the clouds
Warm breeze blows by
Rubbing cheeks like a soft kiss
The sun descending, getting ready for bed
Sad eyes beg to see one more street.
He wags showing his gratitude as we move along

Untitled
By Kendra Law

Will I go somewhere?
Will the blue in my veins red
Will the blood at rest knock my chest
Will the buds if pink bloom my cheeks
Will I climb and will I fall
Will the heavens hum
Will there be the sound of drums
Will the gates be shut
Will I be left to the mutts
Swirling flames
Screaming names
Stuck, stuck, stuck.
Forever it seems
Forever it will be
Will I fall to my knees
Will I scream to be free
Will I jump high
From the one i despise
But remember, we're stuck
Will I raise my hands
Will I praise the heavenly bands
Will I be showered in blood
Will his blood rub
I will now say, not ask
I'm going somewhere
I won't go with the rest

Kristallnacht

By Matthew Ruppenkamp

It was terrible
Just awful
What kind of monster would burn a holy place?
Will everyone just stand idly?

The beautiful glass shattered,
scattered among the ashen rubble.
Something needs doing.
The poor Jews.
More need to help.
Away, they should run;
with returning, their driving fear.
Unbelievable.
So much Knowledge lost.
An entire culture, dying.
Am I the only one;
who tries to do something about this?
If only more people heard the stories;
stories about surviving the prison camps.
Such an impossible achievement,
and so many of my friends have.
I have helped far more than I can count;
but I can never help them all.
I will never forget the families torn apart.
Nor will I stop helping;
until the war is done,

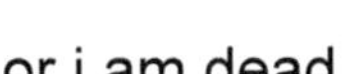

or i am dead.

Beautiful Imperfections

By Marisah Richards

Look into the mirror
See a round face
Big brown eyes staring back
Medium sized eye lashes
Look into the mirror
See that extra chub
The red blemishes everywhere
Look at all those imperfections
Tears trickle down
Leaving nothing but pain
Medium length hair is strewn everywhere
A clump here, a strand there
A curly lock on the left
A ringlet on the right
Look into the mirror
While looking, see everything
All the stuff that could be changed
The round face could be leaner
Big brown eyes could be bluer or greener
Those medium sized lashes could be longer
The hair could be tamer, smoother, less of a mess
The chub could go away
The tears could be gone
The horrible red blemishes could disappear
Look in the mirror
See all of those imperfections
See that crooked smile
The slightly bigger than average nose
Those eyes full of hurt staring back at you
Look in the mirror
Wipe those tears away
You are beautiful!
Those imperfections are what make you beautiful!
That wild mane is what gives you an edge of fierceness
Look at those beautiful almost symmetrical eyes
See those little imperfections
Look in the mirror
See all of those imperfections?
Those imperfections are you!
They make you beautiful!
They set you apart from everyone else
Look in the mirror
See that crooked smile with white teeth showing all their angles
Every little imperfection
Look in the mirror
You are beautiful, imperfections and all

Untitled
By Sidney Petitgout

In my eyes
Why do people stare
Looking you up and down
Giving you nasty looks
As if your a squished up bug found on the ground
Is it cause you have a different colored face?
As if that gives them the right to be mean
Think about it,
In a crayon box
They all are together no matter the color
Is it cause your not the same race?
That doesn't matter to me
Because I can't see
In my eyes
I'm color blind

Untitled

By Kaz Kishiue-Koval

Shaped like cotton candy

Because she's like a vacuum.

Her ears look like they are being pulled up

By strings when a walk is mentioned.

If I'm eating she waits

Like a lion watching its prey.

When she sees water

She turns into a fish.

When she dreams her paws twitch

Like she's chasing rabbis outside.

When I say "Daphne" she always comes to me.

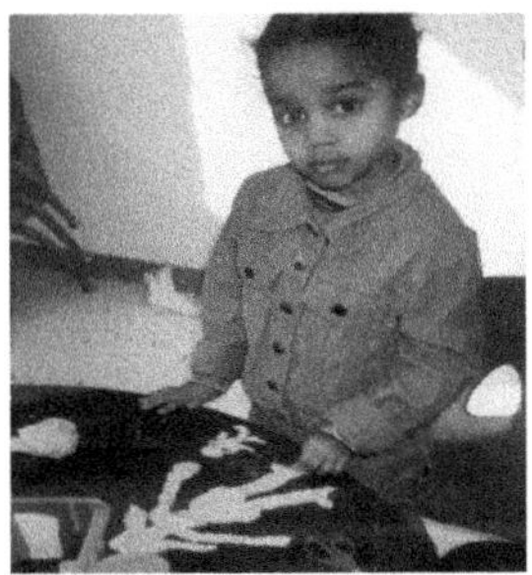

Coal

By Hiba Ibrahim

It's known as the largest organ of the body.
Hers happens to be the color of coal.
Coal, that's what she is,
Tossed around in the fireplace.
The more it burns, the smaller it gets.
The boiling sun over the field of snow.
As she picks up the snowball
It gets spotted in red.

Yet she hums "Wade in the Water,"
Covering up the pain.
It was a mistake, for now she is on the ground
The clanging of the chains getting louder.
She hears a whistle and knows what's coming.
The flesh is now torn.
"Shut the hell up! Did I bring you here to sing?"
"No, Master."

In God We Trust (E Pluribus Unum)

By Hiba Ibrahim

Like zombies we work,

We roam on their land.

Like actors we pretend,

Lost in our two faces.

They, who represent

The house painted white.

The heroes, the patriots,

Blind us and leave us in the dark.

They are seen whispering and cheating

The secrets and lies.

We keep it buried like a corpse.

Not wanting to believe,

Our mouths are sewn shut.

We have quantity,

But the throne they own.

We make the money,

And they are the thieves.

We are the cry.

The media and "official reports"

like a pacifier, keep us quiet.

They keep the truth from the people,

us, who make up this world,

as if it is theirs to keep.

Yet again,

Like zombies we work,

We roam on their land.

Like actors, we pretend,

Lost in our two faces.

We, the weak.

They, the power.

We are all corrupt.

Military

Jarrett Beireis

It's tough to watch him leave
Knowing he may never come home again
Knowing people are trying to kill him
Because
It makes me want to never let him go.
The heartbreak sets in watching him get on the bus
I won't see him in person for at least 2-3 years.
And the sorrows build as each day goes on.

It's tough to watch him leave
Hoping that the phone won't ring
And having someone else say
He has passed away.
But knowing he is doing something courageous and brave
While risking his life doing something honorable.
I count down the days until he returns
But it's almost as if the clocks are frozen.
This is what it's like,
Having your father in the military.

Blind
By Sidney Petitgout

In my eyes
Why do people stare
Looking you up and down
Giving you nasty looks
As if your a squished up bug found on the ground
Is it cause you have a different colored face?
As if that gives them the right to be mean
Think about it,
In a crayon box
They all are together no matter the color
Is it cause your not the same race?
That doesn't matter to me
Because I can't see
In my eyes
I'm color blind

The Low End
By Jaron Lamp

A feeling like nothing before
Playing from one to four
Skipping strings
The joy it brings

The deep rumble
Of nickle vibrations
Captivation at its finest
Fingers pulling strings
Mind pulling fingers
Dreams pulling mind

Too Late
By Jaron Lamp
Left to learn by myself
Lessons of life
Left to learn an example
When none was left

Consumed
In everything
Except what really mattered
Never learned to talk
Always learned to deal
To deal with the things
It's as if stopping gravity

Man who thinks 

By Corey Wieland-Davenport

Man who thinks in blood,

One who never is right,

Creeps an slinks, across the

Floor pulls the knife eyes wide

Mirror of light, spluttery squirt,

Her eyes shown, moonlit gems,

Grow wide, the eyes fade,

Picture in time, recoils to the floor,

Crimson seeps, colors it new, the light in her hair wanes,

Seeped with a darker light, the man stood,

The drip is loud, liquid on liquid,

Drips are faster,

Thoughts run through,

His body shakes,

He chuckles hysterically,

Glow in his eyes, open wide,

Pain flows, metal taste creeps,

To join the tears, chuckles fade,

Coughs and gurgles,

Crimson shined an spoke,

Greeting its new neighbor.

The Night 

By Corey Wieland-Davenport

The laughter, howling to the cheese, keeps me up,

I tried a lot of things to help me sleep

But I can never be rid of it,

When the cheese goes down,

The salmon light from behind fluffy dark,

Picks me up, I feel the dark run,

Light fills me, the dark charges, Terror from outside,

I turn my head, brush the hair from sight,

I feel darker, my hand pains,

Pipes to my heart.

Trying to get up, I hear a scream,

Felt strange sensations, I moved to the door,

The door wasn't locked, Door fell back,

I see a trail of warm colors on the dulled earth,

I follow the trail,

Feeling even more down then I was, The trail seemed to stop,

I looked in shock, see my wife, Color stained her sky dress.

Her beautiful face, Ruined by the pain, I held her hand,

Dark hits heart, I can't hold the tears,

I touch her face, I grab the knife.

The guilt too much, I cry, the new pain pipes to my heart.

I feel sleepy.

Untitled

By: Matthew Ruppenkamp

There are two ways to look at life.
The positive and the negative.
I view life both ways.
Life simply is; no joy in life, no greatness, no unconditional love.
Life is an equal continuum.
Happiness has a price.
There is a goal, my goal. Unattainable, yet I strive.
Two wishes. Small dreams lost in a harsh sea of reality.
To soar through the sky, to fly.
I yearn like a caterpillar for metamorphosis.
Like clothes wish to be worn, I dream to fade.
Disappear and watch.
A guardian angel , but no intervention.
Petty ideals, meaningless whims.
Depressed thoughts.
Sad hoping, internal tearing.
But who would know? No one.
Stonewall façade, a magical gate, not meant to be opened.
I wonder, why? Continue for what? Just keep going. Lets see what happens next
Whose thoughts are these? So strange, foreign and not my own.
They can't be. Or could they be? These sad lonely thoughts.
Filling my head. But why?
This is not me . I mustn't be this way.
Cheer up. Be happy, I have to smile.
The joy within must shine through.

Grandparents Absent
By: Haley Schneider

Glinting blue off the harsh lights
The eye of the elder is captured
Scratch, scratch wax against wood
Childish meaning, meaning more

Blue turns to haze
Glassed over, shiny
A sparkle, extinguished
A kind crinkle, relaxed

One missing out
One too young to remember
One remembering it all
Three feeling the same

Starts with a whine
Next a child,
A lovely time
All to be hushed by a single wail

He takes,
But takes for a reason
The sorrow, that building
Vastness of bareness

You think it will leave
But it's always there
Waiting behind the wall
But for what?

Dream World
Jarrett Beireis

Life is a dream
All fantasy
Where in a perfect world,
In early hours, happiness is served like bacon and eggs
Over easy.
Dream world.

But when a non-blood related semi-stranger teaches you to roll on wheels,
That's when you wake up.
Every family has difficulties.
For example, I've lived with a parent who I don't resemble longer than
I've lived with my biological parents. Total.

New driver, starting to ride solo. Everything I've learned in life,
From riding a bike to driving a car, has come from someone who I'm
Not a replica of. Before I could walk
I never learned how to use the word "Dad"
Until I was 2.

My first memory,
Poverty, hunger, homeless, little clothes.
Newly used feet for the first time
And this is the first thing I remember.

Soon after I was introduced to a new world
And in this new world, the person I have the most affection for,
Suddenly becomes invisible.

Constantly wondering if she's okay.
It's like reaching out to give my hand
Arm too short
And everything fades

I wish it was a dream
But sooner or later,
We all wake up.

Life
By David Jenkins

One chance, No regrets.
Live your life
Enjoy it now
Before you can't later.
Chase your dreams
Few opportunities
Be successful.
Ambition is priceless
Put a vision in your brain
Your legacy may change.
You only live once
If you do it right
That may just be enough.
Grudges threat me everyday
Get over it anyway
Then forgive another day.
One chance, No regrets.

www.ingramcontent.com/pod-product-compliance
Ingram Content Group UK Ltd.
Pitfield, Milton Keynes, MK11 3LW, UK
UKHW051135260726
13967UKWH00010B/3060

9 781312 066441